Supported Employment: The Evidence: Evidence-Based Practices (EBP) KIT

Substance Abuse and Mental Health Services Administration (SAMHSA)

The BiblioGov Project is an effort to expand awareness of the public documents and records of the U.S. Government via print publications. In broadening the public understanding of government and its work, an enlightened democracy can grow and prosper. Ranging from historic Congressional Bills to the most recent Budget of the United States Government, the BiblioGov Project spans a wealth of government information. These works are now made available through an environmentally friendly, print-on-demand basis, using only what is necessary to meet the required demands of an interested public. We invite you to learn of the records of the U.S. Government, heightening the knowledge and debate that can lead from such publications.

Included are the following Collections:

Budget of The United States Government
Presidential Documents
United States Code
Education Reports from ERIC
GAO Reports
History of Bills
House Rules and Manual
Public and Private Laws

Code of Federal Regulations
Congressional Documents
Economic Indicators
Federal Register
Government Manuals
House Journal
Privacy act Issuances
Statutes at Large

EVIDENCE-BASED
PRACTICES
KIT

Knowledge Informing Transformation

The
Evidence

**Supported
Employment**

U.S. DEPARTMENT OF HEALTH AND HUMAN SERVICES
Substance Abuse and Mental Health Services Administration
Center for Mental Health Services
www.samhsa.gov

EVIDENCE-BASED
PRACTICES

KIT

Knowledge Informing Transformation

The
Evidence

**Supported
Employment**

U.S. Department of Health and Human Services
Substance Abuse and Mental Health Services Administration
Center for Mental Health Services

Acknowledgments

This document was produced for the Substance Abuse and Mental Health Services Administration (SAMHSA) by the New Hampshire-Dartmouth Psychiatric Research Center under contract number 280-00-8049 and Westat under contract number 270-03-6005, with SAMHSA, U.S. Department of Health and Human Services (HHS). Neal Brown, M.P.A., and Crystal Blyler, Ph.D., served as the Government Project Officers.

Disclaimer

Public Domain Notice

Electronic Access and Copies of Publication

This publication may be downloaded or ordered at www.samhsa.gov/shin. Or, please call SAMHSA's Health Information Network at **1-877-SAMHSA-7** (1-877-726-4727) (English and Español).

Recommended Citation

Substance Abuse and Mental Health Services Administration. *Supported Employment: The Evidence.* DHHS Pub. No. SMA-08-4364, Rockville, MD: Center for Mental Health Services, Substance Abuse and Mental Health Services Administration, U.S. Department of Health and Human Services, 2009.

Originating Office

Center for Mental Health Services
Substance Abuse and Mental Health Services Administration
1 Choke Cherry Road
Rockville, MD 20857

DHHS Publication No. SMA-08-4364
Printed 2009

EVIDENCE-BASED
PRACTICES

KiT

Knowledge Informing Transformation

The Evidence

The Evidence introduces all stakeholders to the research literature and other resources on Supported Employment. This booklet includes the following resources:

- A document that reviews the research literature,

- A selected bibliography for further reading,

- References for the citations presented throughout the KIT, and

- Acknowledgements of KIT developers and contributors.

Supported Employment

This KIT is part of a series of Evidence-Based Practices KITs created by the Center for Mental Health Services, Substance Abuse and Mental Health Services Administration, U.S. Department of Health and Human Services.

This booklet is part of the Supported Employment KIT that includes a DVD, CD-ROM, and seven booklets:

How to Use the Evidence-Based Practices KITs

Getting Started with Evidence-Based Practices

Building Your Program

Training Frontline Staff

Evaluating Your Program

The Evidence

Using Multimedia to Introduce Your EBP

EVIDENCE-BASED
PRACTICES

KjT

Knowledge Informing Transformation

What's in *The Evidence*

Supported Employment

EVIDENCE-BASED
PRACTICES
KiT

Knowledge Informing Transformation

The Evidence

Review of the Research Literature

A number of research articles summarize the effectiveness of Supported Employment (SE). This KIT includes a full-text copy of one of them:

Bond, G. R., Becker, D. R., Drake, R. E., Rapp, C. A., Meisler, N., Lehman, A. F., et al. (2001). Implementing supported employment as an evidence-based practice, *Psychiatric Services, 52*, 313-322.

This article describes the critical components of the evidence-based model and its effectiveness. Barriers to implementation and strategies for overcoming them are also discussed, based on successful experiences in several states.

You may view this article or print it from the CD-ROM in your KIT. For a printed copy, see page 3.

Implementing Supported Employment as an Evidence-Based Practice

Gary R. Bond, Ph.D.
Deborah R. Becker, M.Ed.
Robert E. Drake, M.D., Ph.D.
Charles A. Rapp, Ph.D.
Neil Meisler, M.S.W.
Anthony F. Lehman, M.D., M.S.P.H.
Morris D. Bell, Ph.D.
Crystal R. Blyler, Ph.D.

2001
Dedicated to
Evidence
Based
Psychiatry

Supported employment for people with severe mental illness is an evidence-based practice, based on converging findings from eight randomized controlled trials and three quasi-experimental studies. The critical ingredients of supported employment have been well described, and a fidelity scale differentiates supported employment programs from other types of vocational services. The effectiveness of supported employment appears to be generalizable across a broad range of client characteristics and community settings. More research is needed on long-term outcomes and on cost-effectiveness. Access to supported employment programs remains a problem, despite their increasing use throughout the United States. The authors discuss barriers to implementation and strategies for overcoming them based on successful experiences in several states. (*Psychiatric Services* 52:313–322, 2000)

As a result of more than two decades of research, we know a great deal about improving outcomes and enhancing the recovery process for persons with severe mental illness by providing effective mental health services. Unfortunately, the implementation of interventions that have been shown to be effective by research, termed here evidence-based practices, lags considerably behind the state of knowledge. Individuals with severe mental disorders such as schizophrenia are unlikely to receive treatment with basic evidence-based practices in routine mental health settings (1). Implementation of evidence-based practices must overcome many obstacles, some generic and some specific to a particular evidence-based practice. Nevertheless, the field of mental health services is slowly committing itself to providing research-based services as the foundation of care (2).

In this paper, the first of several on specific evidence-based practices for persons with severe mental illness, we discuss supported employment, a recent approach to vocational rehabilitation that has proved to be consistently more effective than traditional approaches. Our goals are to familiarize clients, families, clinicians, administrators, and mental health policy makers with supported employment; to review the findings and limitations of current research; and to discuss implementation issues, including availability, barriers, and strategies. Because several recent reviews of research on supported employment already exist (3–7), our intent is to provide information that is accessible to stakeholder groups other than researchers.

Supported employment

Supported employment is a well-defined approach to helping people with disabilities participate as much as possible in the competitive labor market, working in jobs they prefer with the level of professional help they need. According to the federal definition, supported employment means "competitive work in integrated work settings . . . consistent with the strengths, resources, priorities, concerns, abilities, capabilities, interests, and informed choice of the individuals, for individuals with the most significant disabilities for whom competitive employment has not traditionally occurred; or for whom competitive employment has been inter-

Dr. Bond *is affiliated with the department of psychology at Indiana University–Purdue University Indianapolis, 402 North Blackford Street, Indianapolis, Indiana 46202 (e-mail, gbond@iupui.edu).* **Ms. Becker** *and* **Dr. Drake** *are with the New Hampshire–Dartmouth Psychiatric Research Center in Lebanon, New Hampshire.* **Dr. Rapp** *is affiliated with the School of Social Welfare at the University of Kansas in Lawrence.* **Mr. Meisler** *is with the department of psychiatry at the Medical University of South Carolina in Charleston.* **Dr. Lehman** *is with the department of psychiatry at the University of Maryland in Baltimore.* **Dr. Bell** *is with the department of psychiatry at Yale University in New Haven, Connecticut.* **Dr. Blyler** *is affiliated with the Center for Mental Health Services of the Substance Abuse and Mental Health Services Administration in Rockville, Maryland.*

rupted or intermittent as a result of a significant disability" (8).

Although the federal definition of supported employment includes reference to transitional employment, that is, temporary community job placements, the two are very different, both conceptually and in practice (9). Many agencies offer both, and when they do, practitioners understand them to be different approaches; transitional employment is seen as a step toward supported employment (10). We do not discuss transitional employment in this paper.

Although many supported employment principles have been espoused for decades (11), these ideas crystallized in the 1980s through the efforts of a national network of educators, who concluded that sheltered workshops isolate people with developmental disabilities from mainstream society (12). This network was successful in changing federal regulations on the types of services funded by the federal-state vocational rehabilitation system.

By 1987 supported employment had attracted attention in the psychiatric rehabilitation field (13). As adapted for this population, supported employment programs typically provide individual placements in competitive employment—that is, community jobs paying at least minimum wage that any person can apply for—in accord with client choices and capabilities, without requiring extended prevocational training. Unlike other vocational approaches (4,14), supported employment programs do not screen people for work readiness, but help all who say they want to work; they do not provide intermediate work experiences, such as prevocational work units, transitional employment, or sheltered workshops; they actively facilitate job acquisition, often sending staff to accompany clients on interviews; and they provide ongoing support once the client is employed.

Supported employment programs are found in a wide variety of service contexts, including community mental health centers, community rehabilitation programs, clubhouses, and psychiatric rehabilitation centers (10, 15,16). Although the evidence sug-

gests that supported employment is optimally effective only when clients concurrently receive adequate case management, it is not necessarily limited to a specific service model such as assertive community treatment.

The most comprehensively described supported employment approach for people with severe mental illness is the individual placement and support model (17,18). We do not view this approach as a distinct supported employment model. Instead, it is intended as a standardization of supported employment principles in programs for people with severe mental illness, so that supported employment can be clearly described, scientifically studied, and implemented in communities. In fact, a survey of 116 supported employment programs throughout the United States found that these programs generally follow principles of the individual placement and support model (19).

Effectiveness of supported employment

To understand the context of the current review, several points from the broader vocational literature are critical. First, interventions that do not target job placement directly have very little impact on employment outcomes (20). Second, many vocational approaches to helping people with severe mental illness gain employment have been developed over the past half century. Few have been evaluated rigorously; those that have been examined in controlled trials have yielded disappointing results (4,14,21,22).

Quasi-experimental studies. To date, three quasi-experimental studies have evaluated day treatment programs that converted their rehabilitation services to supported employment. Drake and colleagues (23) studied a rural New Hampshire community mental health center that developed a supported employment program to replace the day treatment services. A natural experiment compared the conversion site with a nearby site, which continued its day treatment along with traditional brokered vocational services. The competitive employment rate increased substantially at the conversion site, whereas the rate was unchanged at the com-

parison site. Moreover, adverse outcomes such as hospitalization, incarceration, and dropouts did not increase at the conversion site.

Clients, their families, and mental health staff had favorable reactions to the conversion, although a minority mentioned loss of social contact as a drawback (24). Interestingly, many clients who did not find work also reported that they benefited from the change because they discovered satisfying activities outside the community mental health center.

Replacing day treatment with supported employment also led to cost savings (25). Given the success of the initial conversion, the second site subsequently converted to supported employment with similarly favorable results (26). In a second study involving the downsizing of a day treatment program in a small city, clients who transferred to a new supported employment program had better outcomes than those who remained in day treatment (27).

A third study compared two Rhode Island day treatment programs that converted to supported employment with one that did not (28), with similar findings. Others have also reported successful conversions of day treatment to supported employment programs (29). These evaluations demonstrate that supported employment can be implemented in a cost-effective manner in real-world settings with a broad range of clients with severe mental illness, not just a select group who sign up for supported employment.

Randomized controlled trials. A 1997 review (3) summarized the findings of six randomized controlled trials comparing supported employment with a variety of traditional vocational services for people with severe mental illness (30–35). All six studies reported significant gains in obtaining and keeping employment for persons enrolled in supported employment. For example, a mean of 58 percent of supported employment clients achieved competitive employment at some time over a 12- to 18-month period, compared with 21 percent of the control group, who received a range of alternative vocational interventions, including skills training, sheltered work, and vocational counseling as steps toward competitive job placement. Control subjects received what providers in their communities believed to be best practices in vocational rehabilitation.

Other competitive employment outcomes, such as time employed and employment earnings, also favored supported employment clients over those in control groups. A meta-analysis of these studies reached very similar conclusions, noting that the findings were robust (5,6).

Recently, data collection was completed for the Center for Mental Health Services Employment Intervention Demonstration Program (36). Eight sites in this project used randomized controlled trials to evaluate the effectiveness of supported employment. Reports of findings from this multicenter trial are expected over the next year.

Two sites have reported preliminary experimental findings. In Hartford, Connecticut, Mueser and associates (37) compared individual placement and support with two established vocational approaches. One was a psychiatric rehabilitation center using transitional employment, and the other was a brokered approach using a combination of sheltered workshops, government set-aside jobs, and individual placements. Meisler and colleagues (38) compared an individual placement and support program working within an assertive community treatment team with usual vocational services in a rural community in South Carolina. The control group was assigned to a well-respected rehabilitation center with long-term contracts providing numerous government set-aside jobs.

Findings from both studies replicated the previous findings of large differences in competitive employment outcomes favoring supported employment over traditional approaches. Even with protected jobs—transitional employment and set-aside jobs—factored in, supported employment clients in both studies still had better employment outcomes.

Many of these studies have also examined nonvocational outcomes, such as rehospitalization rates, symptoms, quality of life, and self-esteem. Studies rarely have found any experimental differences in nonvocational outcomes favoring clients enrolled in supported employment programs over those in comparison programs. In other words, the group effects for supported employment programs appear to be restricted mainly to competitive employment outcomes, at least for the relatively brief follow-up periods in the studies reviewed. However, neither has any research suggested any adverse effects from participation in supported employment programs. Rehospitalization rates are unaffected by participation in supported employment, contrary to the belief that the stress of work might lead to higher relapse rates.

Although enrollment in a supported employment program itself does not lead to improved nonvocational outcomes, clients who actually engage in competitive work do experience improvements in self-esteem and in control of symptoms, compared with clients who do not work or work minimally (39,40).

Cost considerations are a core issue in decisions to implement psychiatric services. Supported employment services are labor intensive. Annual cost per supported employment participant is around $2,000 to $4,000 (25,41). These figures are similar to those for traditional vocational services (42). Clients enrolled in supported employment programs sometimes use fewer mental health services, notably day treatment, suggesting a cost offset (25,43–45).

Critical components

Reviewers seeking to identify empirically validated principles of supported employment have reached similar conclusions (7,46–49). Certain components are almost always present in successful vocational programs. They are generally found in the supported employment programs evaluated in the eight randomized controlled trials summarized above. The following components are predictive of better employment outcomes:

♦ The agency providing supported employment services is committed to competitive employment as an attainable goal for its clients with severe mental illness, devoting its resources for rehabilitation services to this endeavor rather than to day treatment or sheltered work. Numerous studies indicate that this element is common in successful programs (23,26–29,33, 34,49,50).

♦ Supported employment programs use a rapid job search approach to help clients obtain jobs directly, rather than providing lengthy preemployment assessment, training, and counseling. The evidence in this area is strong, with two randomized controlled trials focusing specifically on this variable (30,51), plus five randomized controlled trials in which this component was a critical difference between study conditions (32–34,37,38). A randomized controlled trial evaluating a vocational approach involving extended classroom training before job placement yielded employment outcomes similar to those of a control group referred to the state vocational rehabilitation office for vocational services (52).

♦ Staff and clients find individualized job placements according to client preferences, strengths, and work experiences. Several correlational studies support this conclusion (49,53–56).

♦ Follow-along supports are maintained indefinitely. Correlational findings from four different research groups indicate that this component is an important one (31,57–59).

♦ The supported employment program is closely integrated with the mental health treatment team. The experimental evidence is consistent with this conclusion even though this variable has not been studied in isolation (31–33,35,37,38,59). This principle is also supported by a strong theoretical rationale (60). However, despite its strong evidence base, it is not universally practiced (19).

Together these principles serve as a foundation for evidence-based guidelines for providing effective supported employment services. In one statewide survey, programs rated high in implementing these principles had better employment outcomes (unpublished data, Becker DR, 2000). A number of specific program elements—for example, reasonable caseload size, diverse employment settings, assertive outreach, and benefits counseling—are found in most supported employment programs (15), but the association between these elements and better employment outcomes has not yet been established. Further research is needed to clarify the critical ingredients of supported employment, which will lead to modifications, refinements, and additions.

Limitations of the evidence
Client factors
The most consistent finding from the supported employment literature has been the absence of specific client factors predicting better employment outcomes. Diagnosis, symptoms, age, gender, disability status, prior hospitalization, and education have been examined, and none have proved to be strong or consistent predictors (30,32,33). Notably, a co-occurring condition of substance use has not been found to predict employment outcomes (61–63).

Although a work history predicts better employment outcomes in supported employment programs, supported employment remains more effective than traditional vocational services for clients with both good and poor work histories (28,32,33). We speculate that the professional assistance provided by supported employment programs at every stage of the employment process compensates for client deficits in a way that less assertive vocational rehabilitation approaches do not. Consequently, the extensive literature on client predictors of work outcomes among people with severe mental illness who either have had little vocational assistance or have been enrolled in traditional vocational programs (48) may be largely irrelevant for supported employment programs.

Randomized controlled trials of supported employment have been conducted in settings with significant numbers of Caucasian (30–32,59), African-American (33,38), and Latino (37) clients. Although more replications are needed, all the evidence to date suggests that the greater effectiveness of supported employment compared with traditional vocational services is generalizable to both the African-American and Latino popula-

tions. Within-study comparisons of employment rates for different ethnic groups have been hampered by small sample sizes, so we cannot yet determine whether supported employment is equally effective for all ethnic groups within a specific setting.

We may make our best progress in understanding the role of ethnicity in supported employment programs by combining results across studies using meta-analytic techniques and through qualitative studies (64–66). We know anecdotally that culture and language pose significant barriers to providing supported employment in some populations.

Not all clients benefit from supported employment. For example, in community mental health centers converting day treatment programs to supported employment programs, some clients do not have employment as a current goal; not surprisingly, these clients usually do not work. But even among clients who express an interest in working, a sizable proportion are not working at any given time. We need to develop effective strategies for these clients. Helping clients decide whether supported employment is right for them also is critical. Informational sessions explaining beforehand how supported employment works improve clients' ability to make informed decisions about participating, thereby potentially reducing dropout rates (67,68).

Community and economic factors
Supported employment has been implemented successfully in many different types of communities. Programs in rural areas are no less successful than those in urban areas (49,50). One counterintuitive finding is that economic conditions apparently do not have a potent influence on employment rates for a supported employment program (50,69–71). Catalano and colleagues (69) have speculated that an economic theory of labor markets applies here. The primary labor market, comprising professional and semiprofessional jobs, shrinks during economic recessions. The secondary labor market, which includes entry-level jobs in the service industry, is more elastic and less vulnerable to economic down-

turns. Supported employment programs find jobs mostly in this secondary labor market, where jobs are usually available. However, the aforementioned studies examined a relatively restricted range of unemployment. The findings may not be generalizable to communities where the unemployment rate is very high (35).

Job opportunities available to clients with severe mental illness are often restricted because of the clients' limited work experience, education, and training, and consequently most supported employment jobs are unskilled (3,72). Half of all clients leave their supported employment positions within six months (3), although nondisabled workers in these occupations also have high turnover rates (73). Moreover, most supported employment positions are part-time. Clients often limit work hours to avoid jeopardizing Social Security and Medicaid benefits (48,74). A continuing challenge for supported employment programs is helping clients capitalize on educational and training opportunities so that they may qualify for skilled jobs and develop satisfying careers (72).

Program factors
Specific details about the best ways to provide supported employment services have not been adequately researched. Issues include the role of disclosure of mental illness in finding and keeping jobs, the range, location, timing, and intensity of supports provided to clients (57,75), and the nature of coworker and supervisor supports (76). The relationship between supported employment services and medication issues has not been well studied despite its assumed importance (77).

Long-term outcomes of supported employment also have not been widely studied. Programs that remain engaged with their clients over time, respond to clients' expressed wishes, and sustain an approach that integrates clinical and rehabilitation services are those we believe have the best outcomes over time. However, with few exceptions (30,58,59), most randomized controlled trials do not have follow-up information beyond two years. Much longer follow-up periods are needed to determine

316

whether sustained commitment can yield favorable outcomes for more clients.

Implementation barriers
Access to supported employment
Sixty to 70 percent of people with severe mental illness would like to work in competitive employment (78,79), yet 85 percent or more of those in public mental health systems are not doing so (78–82). Most prefer competitive employment to sheltered workshops (83) and day treatment (30,84). However, most clients lack access to employment services of any kind. Less than 25 percent of clients with severe mental illness receive any form of vocational assistance (1,85, 86), and only a fraction of these clients have access to supported employment (87). In some states, supported employment programs are now commonly found in community mental health centers, but their capacity falls far short of the need (19, 50). A further question concerns the quality of available programs. Not surprisingly, it is mixed (15,49).

Barriers to implementation of high-quality programs exist at many levels—within federal, state, and local governments and program or clinic administrations, among clinicians and supervisors, and in the collaboration with clients or families. The remainder of this paper is devoted to discussing the barriers to implementing high-quality supported employment programs and offering suggestions based on experience for overcoming them.

Government barriers
Historically, the federal-state vocational rehabilitation system has been the primary funding source for employment services. However, federal funding for vocational rehabilitation has never been sufficient to serve more than a tiny proportion of the population in need (88). Moreover, many observers have expressed doubts about whether this funding has been used wisely. Vocational rehabilitation expenditures apparently have been disproportionately devoted to administration and to assessment and other preemployment activities (89). Compounding the problem is

the fact that persons with severe mental illness fail to complete the vocational rehabilitation eligibility process twice as often as people with physical disabilities (90). Nevertheless, vocational rehabilitation agencies continue to allocate minimal funding for supported employment services (91).

Public funding for mental health is a second source for financing supported employment services. Unfortunately, community mental health centers historically have allocated only a tiny proportion of their budgets to vocational services (85). Since the 1980s, most states have amended their Medicaid state plans to cover community mental health services under the optional rehabilitative services provision, which permits a broad interpretation of the range of reimbursable interventions.

Vocational training is among the few services statutorily excluded from Medicaid reimbursement. However, evidence-based components of supported employment, such as ongoing supportive counseling in home and community-based settings, team meetings, psychiatrist involvement in rehabilitation planning, and assisting clients in developing job opportunities, are all Medicaid-reimbursed rehabilitative services that states may cover. Yet most state Medicaid plans include unnecessary limitations on covered services when they involve vocational activities. Given the increasing proportion of total funding of community mental health services that Medicaid expenditures represent, misinterpretation of federal Medicaid policy results in a major barrier to supported employment service access.

Fee-for-service systems of reimbursement for units of service, regardless of outcomes, have created incentives to perpetuate services that are not evidence based, such as day treatment (92). Some commentators have concluded that financing of supported employment programs within managed care systems will not be any easier (93).

The fragmentation of supported employment funding has also resulted in separation of services. Historically, supported employment services

have been brokered—that is, offered at an agency separate from the community mental health center (16)—even though we now know that this approach is counterproductive (47, 60). Even supported employment programs that are located in community mental health centers often are not closely integrated with mental health treatment teams (19), despite strong evidence that such integration is vital for success. In Indiana, a separate role for follow-along specialists created by separate funding sources has contributed to discontinuity of services (94).

Directors of state mental health departments can have a critical leadership role in promoting supported employment services. In the 1980s, Ohio's decision to pursue case management and housing as top priorities led to critical improvements, but this decision sacrificed the development of employment services by relegating it to a secondary goal (82). Some states have adopted a "range of vocational options" (95), leading to a proliferation of diverse—and untested—models, whereas other states have invested major resources in specific models that are not evidence based. Still other states have taken the stance that supported employment is not the business of the state mental health agency. Moreover, most states do not systematically monitor client outcomes, precluding the development of objective methods for rewarding successful employment programs.

Program administrators
From an administrator's perspective, common barriers include finding money to finance start-up and ongoing program costs, managing organizational change, and coping with political ramifications of change in the community. Administrators often do not provide the leadership for the adoption of innovations, even when they are evidence based. Administrators who do not have information about evidence-based practices may not value their outcomes or believe that they are possible (49). Administrators, especially those who received training and professional experience in an earlier era, may hold negativist attitudes about the feasibility of

work—for example, "Schizophrenia is a chronic disease with little hope of recovery . . . work is a source of unnecessary stress."

If administrators are unwilling to consider change, it is unlikely that practitioners will. Poor management practices constitute another obvious barrier to implementation of evidence-based practices (96). Agencies that are driven by crises and chaos often have leaders and supervisors who have not established a system of careful treatment planning that is related to clients' desires and needs.

Clinicians and supervisors

Like administrators, clinicians often view clients as too unmotivated to work (97) and often underestimate the need for vocational services (98,99). Many practitioners lack adequate information and skills to staff supported employment programs (100–102).

Resistance to change is a barrier in any organization. In the mental health field, professional identities are defined by what practitioners do—methods employed, program name, and the like—or by their discipline, not by the outcomes sought. Program changes sometimes are introduced as externally imposed ideas rather than resulting from a process that includes the participation of the clinicians and supervisors, who are ultimately responsible for implementing the desired change (103). In such circumstances, practitioners perceive change efforts as a criticism and devaluing of their work.

Another common barrier concerns inadequate resources. Staff members cannot implement supported employment programs effectively if they do not have enough time to carry out their duties or if supervisors give them conflicting messages about the scope of their responsibilities. For example, when employment specialists are assigned additional job duties that are not vocational, they are distracted from the employment effort.

Clients and families

Clients and family members often do not have accurate information about supported employment. Sometimes clients are discouraged from considering employment by well-meaning clinicians and family members who believe that the stress associated with work outweighs the benefits. Instead, they are directed to day programs. Clients often believe that returning to work automatically compromises their eligibility for Social Security and Medicaid benefits. Families may not be given information on how to support a family member's work efforts, or they may not be considered part of the team or support network.

Strategies for implementation

Although we have more systematic information about barriers to evidence-based practices than we do about strategies to overcome them, some approaches for implementing evidence-based practices have been identified (104,105).

Government efforts

At the state level, a first step is to set clear outcome priorities. Next, systematic assessment of employment outcomes is absolutely essential. State mental health authorities must remove organizational and financial barriers to the development of supported employment programs, as has been done in New Hampshire (50), Vermont (unpublished data, Dalmasse D, 1998), Rhode Island (106), and Kansas (49). In both New Hampshire and Rhode Island, state mental health and Medicaid agencies joined to request that the Health Care Financing Administration allow reimbursement for supported employment services aside from direct interventions to teach job skills. Their requests were approved, thereby enabling Medicaid financing to greatly increase clients' access to supported employment services.

Recent federal legislation—the Medicaid buy-in program authorized by the Balanced Budget Act of 1997 and the Ticket to Work and Work Incentives Improvement Act of 1999—has permitted state governments more flexibility in establishing Medicaid eligibility, with the intent of reducing barriers to employment posed by the potential loss of Medicaid benefits (107). Some states—Oregon and Minnesota, for example—have implemented new policies expanding Medicaid coverage to allow more liberal income and resource thresholds for people with disabilities who work.

State mental health authorities have had success in providing direct incentives to local systems for meeting employment goals. In Ohio, participating systems doubled their employment rate when incentives were instituted (82). In New Hampshire, the competitive employment rate for community mental health center clients with severe mental illness has increased from 7 percent to 37 percent since 1990, when the state began emphasizing competitive employment in contracting (50). State vocational rehabilitation agencies in Alabama, Oklahoma, and Pennsylvania have initiated "results-based funding" for supported employment, which similarly rewards agencies for performance (108,109). Some caution is necessary, because unless designed carefully, such incentive systems may encourage enrolling clients with the fewest needs.

Incentives are not enough, however. The state agencies should also take the leadership in providing technical assistance by forming partnerships with leading research and training centers with appropriate expertise, as have those of New Hampshire (110), Rhode Island (106), and other states. Kansas, Indiana, New Jersey, and New York City have established supported employment technical assistance centers to help local programs implement and monitor supported employment services.

Building consensus among stakeholders is another element in the adoption of evidence-based practices. The National Association of State Mental Health Program Directors has issued a position statement on employment and rehabilitation for persons with severe psychiatric disabilities that identifies state mental health agencies as having a responsibility to influence vocational rehabilitation and other state employment agencies to collaborate to improve access by persons with severe mental illness to competitive employment (111). Accepting this mandate, Rhode Island's state mental health agency has involved the state's Medicaid and vocational rehabilitation agencies in funding supported employment.

Funding for consensus-building activities related to exemplary practices is available through the Community Action Grant Program of the Center for Mental Health Services.

Efforts of program administrators
High-achieving organizations concentrate energy and resources on specific outcomes and reduce distractions to those outcomes (112). Important elements of leadership include articulating desired outcomes and practices for achieving them, building an organizational structure and culture that will facilitate implementing evidence-based practices, designing systems to monitor evidence-based practices and client outcomes, hiring staff with appropriate attitudes and skills, establishing group supervision or other methods of collaboration, creating employee evaluation procedures that emphasize evidence-based practices and employment outcomes, and providing rewards for high performance in those areas (49,113).

Supported employment programs are most successful in agencies that make a total commitment to competitive employment without diluting their focus and resources with traditional forms of vocational programming (49,50). A similar pattern is found in the developmental disability field, where supported employment has failed to develop its full potential because many agencies have viewed supported employment as an "add-on" service while maintaining large sheltered workshops (114).

As noted above, community mental health centers have been successful in converting day treatment programs completely to supported employment. Because this redeployment of resources has the advantage of cost savings in addition to acceptance by important stakeholders, it is a very appealing strategy. Consumer-run services can play a role in meeting the social needs of unemployed clients after conversion from day treatment to supported employment (115).

Monitoring the fidelity of program implementation is critical for implementing evidence-based practices (116). Accordingly, researchers, state planners, program directors, clients, and family members are increasingly emphasizing fidelity. The Individual Placement and Support Fidelity Scale (117), a 15-item instrument that assesses the implementation of critical ingredients of supported employment, is one such tool in the public domain. Although it was designed for use by assessors who are familiar with the critical ingredients of the model, its simplicity permits its use by nonresearchers.

Adequate reliability has been found in a field test using site visits by pairs of assessors who interviewed staff, studied charts, and observed program activities (117). The Individual Placement and Support Fidelity Scale clearly differentiates supported employment programs from other vocational approaches, suggesting that it can be used to determine whether a program actually is implementing supported employment (19). More comprehensive scales measuring supported employment implementation also have been field-tested (15,94).

Efforts of clinicians and supervisors
Agencies that successfully adopt supported employment appear to share a set of common elements (49,113, 118). Successful programs give staff the resources they need to do their job well. This also means that the agency itself must be well managed in other areas and must provide high-quality case management services. Supervisors need to provide clear vision, organize services into a multidisciplinary team structure, and focus on outcomes rather than service units and paperwork (119).

Community mental health centers successfully adopting an innovation usually have at least one key change agent who champions the innovation (120). The change agent must have sufficient authority to implement change. When introducing supported employment, the change agent identifies respected frontline practitioners who can help lead the implementation effort. They in turn recruit other staff to join in the planning and development of the new program so that all staff will feel ownership of the program.

Adequate training and ongoing supervision are critical to give staff the skills to implement the practice (118).

Guidelines, training manuals, and videotapes are important tools for ongoing monitoring and transmission of the culture of the supported employment program (118). Another critical element is expert consultation through site visits and telephone conference calls. Implementation is facilitated by having staff—not just employment specialists but also administrators, clinicians, and supervisors—visit exemplary supported employment programs.

Efforts of clients and families
Clients and families are well aware of the need for vocational services (89,98,121) but need to know what good services look like and how to advocate effectively in legislation and funding decisions. They can have influence over setting standards and ensuring adherence to those standards at the state, program, and client levels. Clients and family members should seek membership on advisory boards at all levels. They can collaborate with state officials to fund supported employment programs and to establish standards based on evidence-based practices and have them incorporated in licensing standards, requests for proposals for grant funds, and so on. At the program level, they can demand that entrance criteria for supported employment be based on a client's desire to work and not on symptoms or work history. They can also participate in designing supported employment programs. On an individual client level, they can argue for client choice and services that match evidence-based practices.

Conclusions
The emerging evidence base on supported employment is clear and consistent, with improved employment outcomes across many different types of settings and populations. In addition, most supported employment approaches described in the literature converge on a set of critical components.

One key remaining task is to overcome implementation barriers to make supported employment services available on a widespread basis. No other vocational rehabilitation approach for people with severe mental illness has attained the status of evidence-based practice despite a half century of program innovation and informal experimentation by many psychiatric rehabilitation programs. Proponents of other vocational approaches either have failed to empirically investigate their methods or have failed to find strong evidence. It is also true that many vocational program approaches that are not effective continue to be widely practiced.

Beyond implementing supported employment, we must continue to refine and improve our model to reach a wider spectrum of the population and to help clients not only find and keep paid community jobs but also to develop long-term careers.

Acknowledgments

Work on this paper was supported by National Institute of Mental Health grants MH-00842 and MH-00839, Center for Mental Health Services contract 280-00-8049, and a grant from the Robert Wood Johnson Foundation.

References

1. Lehman AF, Steinwachs DM: Patterns of usual care for schizophrenia: initial results from the Schizophrenia Patient Outcomes Research Team (PORT) client survey. Schizophrenia Bulletin 24:11–23, 1998

2. Drake RE, Goldman HH, Leff HS, et al: Implementing evidence-based practices in routine mental health service settings. Psychiatric Services 52:179–182, 2001

3. Bond GR, Drake RE, Mueser KT, et al: An update on supported employment for people with severe mental illness. Psychiatric Services 48:335–346, 1997

4. Bond GR, Drake RE, Becker DR, et al: Effectiveness of psychiatric rehabilitation approaches for employment of people with severe mental illness. Journal of Disability Policy Studies 10(1):18–52, 1999

5. Crowther R, Marshall M, Bond GR, et al: Vocational rehabilitation for people with severe mental disorders. Cochrane Review, in Cochrane Library. Oxford, England, Update Software, in press

6. Crowther RE, Marshall M, Bond GR, et al: Helping people with severe mental illness to return to work: a systematic review. British Medical Journal, in press

7. Ridgway P, Rapp C: The Active Ingredients in Achieving Competitive Employment for People With Psychiatric Disabilities: A Research Synthesis. Lawrence, University of Kansas, School of Social Welfare, 1998

8. Rehabilitation Act Amendments of 1998: Title IV of the Workforce Investment Act of 1998, Pub Law 105-220, 112 Stat 936

9. Bilby R: A response to the criticisms of transitional employment. Psychosocial Rehabilitation Journal 16(2):69–82, 1992

10. Picone J, Drake RE, Becker D, et al: A survey of clubhouse programs. Indianapolis, Indiana University Purdue University Indianapolis, Department of Psychology, 1998

11. Newman L: Instant placement: a new model for providing rehabilitation services within a community mental health program. Community Mental Health Journal 6:401–410, 1970

12. Wehman P: Supported competitive employment for persons with severe disabilities. Journal of Applied Rehabilitation Counseling 17:24–29, 1986

13. Mellen V, Danley K: Special issue: Supported Employment for Persons with Severe Mental Illness. Psychosocial Rehabilitation Journal 9(2):1–102, 1987

14. Bond GR: Vocational rehabilitation, in Handbook of Psychiatric Rehabilitation. Edited by Liberman RP. New York, Macmillan, 1992

15. Bond GR, Picone J, Mauer B, et al: The Quality of Supported Employment Implementation Scale. Journal of Vocational Rehabilitation 14:201–212, 2000

16. Gervey R, Parrish A, Bond GR: Survey of exemplary supported employment programs for persons with psychiatric disabilities. Journal of Vocational Rehabilitation 5:115–125, 1995

17. Becker DR, Drake RE: A Working Life: The Individual Placement and Support (IPS) Program. Concord, NH, New Hampshire–Dartmouth Psychiatric Research Center, 1993

18. Drake RE, Becker DR: The individual placement and support model of supported employment. Psychiatric Services 47:473–475, 1996

19. Bond GR, Vogler KM, Resnick SG, et al: Dimensions of supported employment: factor structure of the IPS Fidelity Scale. Journal of Mental Health, in press

20. Vandergoot D: Review of placement research literature: implications for research and practice. Rehabilitation Counseling Bulletin 30:243–272, 1987

21. Baronet A, Gerber GJ: Psychiatric rehabilitation: efficacy of four models. Clinical Psychology Review 18:189–228, 1998

22. Lehman AF: Vocational rehabilitation in schizophrenia. Schizophrenia Bulletin 21:645–656, 1995

23. Drake RE, Becker DR, Biesanz JC, et al: Rehabilitation day treatment vs supported employment: I. vocational outcomes. Community Mental Health Journal 30:519–532, 1994

24. Torrey WC, Becker DR, Drake RE: Rehabilitative day treatment versus supported employment: II. consumer, family, and staff reactions to a program change. Psychosocial Rehabilitation Journal 18(3):67–75, 1995

25. Clark RE: Supported employment and managed care: can they co-exist? Psychiatric Rehabilitation Journal 22(1):62–68, 1998

26. Drake RE, Becker DR, Biesanz JC, et al: Day treatment versus supported employment for persons with severe mental illness: a replication study. Psychiatric Services 47:1125–1127, 1996

27. Bailey EL, Ricketts SK, Becker DR, et al: Do long-term day treatment clients benefit from supported employment? Psychiatric Rehabilitation Journal 22(1):24–29, 1998

28. Becker DR, Bond GR, McCarthy D, et al: Converting day treatment centers to supported employment programs in Rhode Island. Psychiatric Services 52:351–357, 2001

29. Gold M, Marrone J: Mass Bay Employment Services (a service of Bay Cove Human Services, Inc): a story of leadership, vision, and action resulting in employment for people with mental illness, in Roses and Thorns from the Grassroots. Boston, Institute of Community Action, 1998

30. Bond GR, Dietzen LL, McGrew JH, et al: Accelerating entry into supported employment for persons with severe psychiatric disabilities. Rehabilitation Psychology 40:91–111, 1995

31. Chandler D, Meisel J, Hu T, et al: A capitated program for a cross-section of severely mentally ill clients: employment outcomes. Community Mental Health Journal 33:501–516, 1997

32. Drake RE, McHugo GJ, Becker DR, et al: The New Hampshire study of supported employment for people with severe mental illness: vocational outcomes. Journal of Consulting and Clinical Psychology 64:391–399, 1996

33. Drake RE, McHugo GJ, Bebout RR, et al: A randomized clinical trial of supported employment for inner-city patients with severe mental illness. Archives of General Psychiatry 56:627–633, 1999

34. Gervey R, Bedell JR: Supported employment in vocational rehabilitation, in Psychological Assessment and Treatment of Persons With Severe Mental Disorders. Edited by Bedell JR. Washington, DC, Taylor & Francis, 1994

35. McFarlane WR, Dushay RA, Deakins SM, et al: Employment outcomes in family-aided assertive community treatment. American Journal of Orthopsychiatry 70:203–214, 2000

36. Carey MA: The continuing need for research on vocational rehabilitation programs. Psychosocial Rehabilitation Journal 18(4):163–164, 1995

37. Mueser KT, Clark RE, Drake RE, et al: A comparison of the individual placement and support model with the psychosocial rehabilitation approach to vocational rehabilitation for consumers with severe mental illness: the results of a controlled trial. Presented at the Fourth Biennial Research Seminar on Work, Matrix Research Institute, Philadelphia, Oct 11–13, 2000

38. Meisler N, Williams O, Kelleher J, et al: Rural-based supported employment approaches: results from South Carolina site of the Employment Intervention Demonstration Project. Presented at the Fourth

Biennial Research Seminar on Work, Matrix Research Institute, Philadelphia, Oct 11–13, 2000

39. Bond GR, Resnick SR, Drake RE, et al: Does competitive employment improve nonvocational outcomes for people with severe mental illness? Journal of Consulting and Clinical Psychology, in press

40. Mueser KT, Becker DR, Torrey WC, et al: Work and nonvocational domains of functioning in persons with severe mental illness: a longitudinal analysis. Journal of Nervous and Mental Disease 185:419–426, 1997

41. Kregel J, Wehman P, Revell G, et al: Supported employment benefit-cost analysis: preliminary findings. Journal of Vocational Rehabilitation 14:153–161, 2000

42. Clark RE, Bond GR: Costs and benefits of vocational programs for people with serious mental illness, in Schizophrenia. Edited by Moscarelli M, Rupp A, Sartorius N. Sussex, England, Wiley, 1996

43. Bond GR, Dietzen LL, Vogler KM, et al: Toward a framework for evaluating costs and benefits of psychiatric rehabilitation: three case examples. Journal of Vocational Rehabilitation 5:75–88, 1995

44. Clark RE, Xie H, Becker DR, et al: Benefits and costs of supported employment from three perspectives. Journal of Behavioral Health Services and Research 25:22–34, 1998

45. Rogers ES, Sciarappa K, MacDonald-Wilson K, et al: A benefit-cost analysis of a supported employment model for persons with psychiatric disabilities. Evaluation and Program Planning 18:105–115, 1995

46. Bond GR: Applying psychiatric rehabilitation principles to employment: recent findings, in Schizophrenia: Exploring the Spectrum of Psychosis. Edited by Ancill RJ, Holliday S, Higenbottam J. Chichester, England, Wiley, 1994

47. Bond GR: Principles of the individual placement and support model: empirical support. Psychiatric Rehabilitation Journal 22(1):11–23, 1998

48. Cook J, Razzano L: Vocational rehabilitation for persons with schizophrenia: recent research and implications for practice. Schizophrenia Bulletin 26:87–103, 2000

49. Gowdy EA: "Work Is the Best Medicine I Can Have": Identifying Best Practices in Supported Employment for People With Psychiatric Disabilities. Ph.D. dissertation. Lawrence, University of Kansas, School of Social Welfare, 2000

50. Drake RE, Fox TS, Leather PK, et al: Regional variation in competitive employment for persons with severe mental illness. Administration and Policy in Mental Health 25:493–504, 1998

51. Bond GR, Dincin J: Accelerating entry into transitional employment in a psychosocial rehabilitation agency. Rehabilitation Psychology 31:143–155, 1986

52. Rogers ES: A randomized controlled study of psychiatric vocational rehabilitation services. Presented at the Fourth Biennial Research Seminar on Work, Matrix Research Institute, Philadelphia, Oct 11–13, 2000

53. Abrams K, DonAroma P, Karan OC: Consumer choice as a predictor of job satisfaction and supervisor ratings for people with disabilities. Journal of Vocational Rehabilitation 9:205–215, 1997

54. Becker DR, Drake RE, Farabaugh A, et al: Job preferences of clients with severe psychiatric disorders participating in supported employment programs. Psychiatric Services 47:1223–1226, 1996

55. Gervey R, Kowal H: A description of a model for placing youth and young adults with psychiatric disabilities in competitive employment. Presented at the International Association of Psychosocial Rehabilitation Services Conference, Albuquerque, May 9–13, 1994

56. Mueser KT, Becker DR, Wolfe R: Supported employment, job preferences, and job tenure and satisfaction. Journal of Mental Health, in press

57. Cook JA, Razzano L: Natural vocational supports for persons with severe mental illness: thresholds supported competitive employment program. New Directions for Mental Health Services, no 56:23–41, 1992

58. McHugo GJ, Drake RE, Becker DR: The durability of supported employment effects. Psychiatric Rehabilitation Journal 22(1):55–61, 1998

59. Test MA, Allness DJ, Knoedler WH: Impact of seven years of assertive community treatment. Presented at the American Psychiatric Association Institute on Psychiatric Services, Boston, Oct 6–10, 1995

60. Drake RE, Becker DR, Xie H, et al: Barriers in the brokered model of supported employment for persons with psychiatric disabilities. Journal of Vocational Rehabilitation 5:141–150, 1995

61. Goldberg RW, Lucksted A, McNary S, et al: Correlates of long-term unemployment among inner-city adults with serious and persistent mental illness. Psychiatric Services 52:101–103, 2001

62. Meisler N, Blankertz L, Santos AB, et al: Impact of assertive community treatment on homeless persons with co-occurring severe psychiatric and substance use disorders. Community Mental Health Journal 33:113–122, 1997

63. Sengupta A, Drake RE, McHugo GJ: The relationship between substance use disorder and vocational functioning among persons with severe mental illness. Psychiatric Rehabilitation Journal 22(1):41–45, 1998

64. Alverson H, Vicente E: An ethnographic study of vocational rehabilitation for Puerto Rican Americans with severe mental illness. Psychiatric Rehabilitation Journal 22(1):69–72, 1998

65. Harris M, Bebout RR, Freeman DW, et al: Work stories: psychological responses to work in a population of dually diagnosed adults. Psychiatric Quarterly 68:131–153, 1997

66. Quimby E, Drake RE, Becker DR: Ethnographic findings from the Washington, DC, Vocational Services Study. Psychiatric Rehabilitation Journal, in press

67. Bebout RR, Becker DR, Drake RE: A research induction group for clients entering a mental health research project: a replication study. Community Mental Health Journal 34:289–295, 1998

68. Drake RE, Becker DR, Anthony WA: The use of a research induction group in mental health services research. Hospital and Community Psychiatry 45:487–489, 1994

69. Catalano R, Drake RE, Becker DR, et al: Labor market conditions and employment of the mentally ill. Journal of Mental Health Policy and Economics 2:51–54, 1999

70. Gowdy EA, Rapp CA, Coffman M, et al: The relationship between economic conditions and employment of people with severe and persistent mental illness. Lawrence, University of Kansas, School of Social Welfare, 2000

71. Purlee GD: Predictors of Employment Outcome for Persons With Serious Mental Illness. Ph.D. dissertation. Bloomington, Indiana University, School of Education, 1993

72. Baron R, Salzer MS: The career patterns of persons with serious mental illness: generating a new vision of lifetime careers for those in recovery. Psychiatric Rehabilitation Skills 4:136–156, 2000

73. Adams-Shollenberger GE, Mitchell TE: A comparison of janitorial workers with mental retardation and their non-disabled peers on retention and absenteeism. Journal of Rehabilitation 62(3):56–60, 1996

74. Averett S, Warner R, Little J, et al: Labor supply, disability benefits, and mental illness. Eastern Economic Journal 25:279–288, 1999

75. Rogers ES, MacDonald-Wilson K, Danley K, et al: A process analysis of supported employment services for persons with serious psychiatric disability: implications for program design. Journal of Vocational Rehabilitation 8:233–242, 1997

76. Rollins AL, Bond GR, Salyers MP: Interpersonal relationships on the job: does the employment program make a difference? Presented at the Fourth Biennial Research Seminar on Work, Matrix Research Institute, Philadelphia, Oct 11–13, 2000

77. Bond GR, Meyer PS: The role of medications in the employment of people with schizophrenia. Journal of Rehabilitation 65(4):9–16, 1999

78. Mueser KT, Salyers MP, Mueser PR: A prospective analysis of work in schizophrenia. Schizophrenia Bulletin, in press

79. Rogers ES, Walsh D, Masotta L, et al: Massachusetts Survey of Client Preferences for Community Support Services (final report). Boston, Boston University, Center for Psychiatric Rehabilitation, 1991

80. Anthony WA, Blanch A: Supported employment for persons who are psychiatrically disabled: an historical and conceptual perspective. Psychosocial Rehabilitation Journal 11(2):5–23, 1987

81. Henry GT: Practical Sampling. Newbury Park, Calif, Sage, 1990

82. Hogan MF: Supported Employment: How Can Mental Health Leaders Make a Difference? Columbus, Ohio Department of Mental Health, 1999

83. Bedell JR, Draving D, Parrish A, et al: A description and comparison of experiences of people with mental disorders in supported employment and paid prevocational training. Psychiatric Rehabilitation Journal 21(3):279–283, 1998

84. Hatfield AB: Serving the unserved in community rehabilitation programs. Psychosocial Rehabilitation Journal 13(2):71–82, 1989

85. Hollingsworth EJ, Sweeney JK: Mental health expenditures for services for people with severe mental illness. Psychiatric Services 48:485–490, 1997

86. Leff HS, Wise M: Measuring service system implementation in a public mental health system through provider descriptions of employment service need and use. Psychosocial Rehabilitation Journal 18(4): 51–64, 1995

87. Five State Feasibility Study on State Mental Health Agency Performance Measures: Draft Executive Summary. Alexandria, Va, National Association of State Mental Health Program Directors Research Institute, Inc, 1998

88. Wehman P, Moon MS: Vocational Rehabilitation and Supported Employment. Baltimore, Brookes, 1988

89. Noble JH, Honberg RS, Hall LL, et al: A Legacy of Failure: The Inability of the Federal-State Vocational Rehabilitation System to Serve People With Severe Mental Illness. Arlington, Va, National Alliance for the Mentally Ill, 1997

90. Marshak LE, Bostick D, Turton LJ: Closure outcomes for clients with psychiatric disabilities served by the vocational rehabilitation system. Rehabilitation Counseling Bulletin 33:247–250, 1990

91. Wehman P, Revell G: Supported employment: a decade of rapid growth and impact. American Rehabilitation 24(1):31–43, 1998

92. Riggs RT: HMOs and the seriously mentally ill: a view from the trenches. Community Mental Health Journal 32:213–218, 1996

93. Baron RC, Rutman ID, Hadley T: Rehabilitation services for people with long-term mental illness in the managed behavioral health care system: stepchild again? Psychiatric Rehabilitation Journal 20(2):33–38, 1996

94. Vogler KM: A Fidelity Study of the Indiana Supported Employment Model for Individuals With Severe Mental Illness. Ph.D. dissertation. Indianapolis, Indiana University–Purdue University Indianapolis, Department of Psychology, 1998

95. Barton R: Psychosocial rehabilitation services in community support systems: a review of outcomes and policy recommendations. Psychiatric Services 50:525–534, 1999

96. McDonnell J, Nofs D, Hardman M, et al: An analysis of the procedural components of supported employment programs associated with employment outcomes. Journal of Applied Behavior Analysis 22:417–428, 1989

97. Braitman A, Counts P, Davenport R, et al: Comparison of barriers to employment for unemployed and employed clients in a case management program: an exploratory study. Psychiatric Rehabilitation Journal 19(1):3–18, 1995

98. Crane-Ross D, Roth D, Lauber BG: Consumers' and case managers' perceptions of mental health and community support service needs. Community Mental Health Journal 36:161–178, 2000

99. Spaniol L, Jung H, Zipple AM, et al: Families as a resource in the rehabilitation of the severely psychiatrically disabled, in Families of the Mentally Ill: Coping and Adaptation. Edited by Hatfield AB, Lefley HP. New York, Guilford, 1987

100. Gill KJ, Pratt CW, Barrett N: Preparing psychiatric rehabilitation specialists through undergraduate education. Community Mental Health Journal 33:323–329, 1997

101. Noble JH: The benefits and costs of supported employment for people with mental illness and with traumatic brain injury in New York State. Buffalo, Research Foundation of the State University of New York, 1991

102. Shafer MS, Pardee R, Stewart M: An assessment of the training needs of rehabilitation and community mental health workers in a six-state region. Psychiatric Rehabilitation Journal 23(2):161–169, 1999

103. Corrigan PW, McCracken SG: Interactive Staff Training: Rehabilitation Teams That Work. New York, Plenum, 1997

104. Addiction Technology Transfer Center: The Change Book: A Blueprint for Technology Transfer. Rockville, Md, Addiction Technology Transfer Center National Network, 2000

105. Torrey WC, Drake RE, Dixon L, et al: Implementing evidence-based practices for persons with severe mental illness. Psychiatric Services 52:45–50, 2001

106. McCarthy D, Thompson D, Olson S: Planning a statewide project to convert day treatment to supported employment. Psychiatric Rehabilitation Journal 22(1): 30–33, 1998

107. Golden TP, O'Mara S, Ferrell C, et al: A theoretical construct for benefits planning and assistance, in the Ticket to Work and Work Incentive Improvement Act. Journal of Vocational Rehabilitation 14:147–152, 2000

108. Brooke V, Green H, O'Brien D, et al: Supported employment: it's working in Alabama. Journal of Vocational Rehabilitation 14:163–171, 2000

109. Novak J, Mank D, Revell G, et al: Paying for success: results-based approaches to funding supported employment, in Supported Employment in Business: Expanding the Capacity of Workers With Disabilities. Edited by Wehman P. St Augustine, Fla, Training Resource Network, in press

110. Bridging Science and Service: A Report by the National Advisory Mental Health Council's Clinical Treatment and Services Research Workgroup. Rockville, Md, National Institute of Mental Health, 1999

111. Position statement on employment and rehabilitation for persons with severe psychiatric disabilities. National Association of State Mental Health Program Directors, 1996. Available at www.nasmhpd.org/employps.htm

112. Batalden PB, Stoltz PK: A framework for the continual improvement of health care: building and applying professional and improvement knowledge to test changes in daily work. Joint Commission 19:424–435, 1993

113. Becker DR, Torrey WC, Toscano R, et al: Building recovery-oriented services: lessons from implementing individual placement and support (IPS) in community mental health centers. Psychiatric Rehabilitation Journal 22(1):51–61, 1998

114. Mank D: The underachievement of supported employment: a call for reinvestment. Journal of Disability Policy Studies 5(2):1–24, 1994

115. Torrey WC, Mead S, Ross G: Addressing the social needs of mental health consumers when day treatment programs convert to supported employment: can consumer-run services play a role? Psychiatric Rehabilitation Journal 22(1):73–75, 1998

116. Bond GR, Evans L, Salyers MP, et al: Measurement of fidelity in psychiatric rehabilitation. Mental Health Services Research 2:75–87, 2000

117. Bond GR, Becker DR, Drake RE, et al: A fidelity scale for the individual placement and support model of supported employment. Rehabilitation Counseling Bulletin 40:265–284, 1997. Instrument available at www.vcu.edu/rrtcweb/sec/outcomes.html

118. Milne D, Gorenski O, Westerman C, et al: What does it take to transfer training? Psychiatric Rehabilitation Skills 4:259–281, 2000

119. Rapp C, Poertner J: Social Administration: A Client-Centered Approach. White Plains, NY, Longman, 1992

120. Backer T, Liberman R, Kuehnel T: Dissemination and adoption of innovative psychosocial interventions. Journal of Consulting and Clinical Psychology 54: 111–118, 1986

121. Steinwachs DM, Kasper JD, Skinner EA: Family Perspectives on Meeting the Needs for Care of Severely Mentally Ill Relatives: A National Survey. Baltimore, Johns Hopkins University, Center on the Organization and Financing of Care for the Severely Mentally Ill, 1992

EVIDENCE-BASED
PRACTICES
KjT

Knowledge Informing Transformation

The Evidence

Selected Bibliography

Evidence from the Employment Intervention Demonstration Program

Employment Intervention Demonstration Program (EIDP) was a 5-year, eight-site, randomized study sponsored by the SAMHSA's Center for Mental Health Services to better understand the most effective ways to help consumers find and keep jobs. With more than 1,400 participants, it was the largest, most comprehensive study of vocational services for people with serious mental illnesses at the time of printing. The following articles published in professional journals represent the most high-quality, recent information available resulting from this landmark study.

Burke-Miller, J. K., Cook, J. A., Grey, D. D., Razzano, L. A., Blyler, C. R., Leff, H. S., et al. (2006). Demographic characteristics and employment among people with severe mental illness in a multisite study. *Community Mental Health Journal, 42,* 143-159.

Cook, J. A., Blyler, C. R., Leff, H. S., McFarlane, W. R., Goldberg, R. W., Gold, P. B., et al. (2008). The Employment Intervention Demonstration Program: Major findings and policy implications. *Psychiatric Rehabilitation Journal, 31,* 291-295.

Cook, J. A., Blyler, C. R., McFarlane, W. R., Leff, H. S., Mueser, K. T., Gold, P. B., et al. (in press). Effectiveness of supported employment for individuals with schizophrenia: Results of a multi-site randomized trial. *Clinical Schizophrenia & Related Psychoses.*

Cook, J. A., Leff, H. S., Blyler, C. R., Gold, P. B., Goldberg, R. W., Clark, R. E., et al. (2006). Estimated payments to employment service providers for persons with mental illness in the Ticket to Work program. *Psychiatric Services, 57,* 465-471.

Cook, J. A., Lehman, A. F., Drake, R., McFarlane, W. R., Gold, P. B., Leff, H. S., et al. (2005) Integration of psychiatric and vocational services: A multisite randomized, controlled trial of supported employment. *American Journal of Psychiatry, 162,* 1948-1956.

Cook, J. A., Mulkern, V., Grey, D. D., Burke-Miller, J., Blyler, C. R., Razzano, L. A., et al. (2006). Effects of local unemployment rate on vocational outcomes in a randomized trial of supported employment for individuals with psychiatric disabilities. *Journal of Vocational Rehabilitation, 25,* 71-84.

Cook, J. A., Razzano, L. A., Burke-Miller, J. K., Blyler, C. R., Leff, H. S., Mueser, K. T., et al. (2007). Effects of co-occurring disorders on employment outcomes in a multi-site randomized study of supported employment for people with severe mental illness. *Journal of Rehabilitation Research and Development, 44,* 837-850.

Gold, P. B., Meisler, N., Santos, A. B., Carnemolla, M. A., Williams, O. H., & Keleher, J. (2006). Randomized trial of supported employment integrated with Assertive Community Treatment for rural adults with severe mental illness. *Schizophrenia Bulletin, 32,* 378-395.

Leff, H. S., Cook, J. A., Gold, P. B., Toprac, M., Blyler, C., Goldberg, R. W, et al. (2005). Effects of job development and job support on competitive employment of persons with severe mental illness. *Psychiatric Services, 56,* 1237-1244.

Lehman, A. F., Goldberg, R., Dixon, L. B., McNary, S., Postrado, L., Hackman, A., et al. (2002). Improving employment outcomes for persons with severe mental illnesses. *Archives of General Psychiatry, 59,* 165-172.

Macias, C., DeCarlo, L. T., Wang, Q., Frey, J., & Barreira, P. (2001). Work interest as a predictor of competitive employment: Policy implications for psychiatric rehabilitation. *Administration and Policy in Mental Health, 28*(4), 279-297.

Macias, C., Rodican, C. F., Hargreaves, W. A., Jones, D. R., Barreira, P. J., & Wang, Q. (2006). Supported employment outcomes of a randomized controlled trial of ACT and clubhouse models. *Psychiatric Services, 57,* 1406–1415.

Mueser, K. T., Clark, R. E., Haines, M., Drake, R. E., McHugo, G. J., Bond, G. R., et al. (2004). The Hartford study of supported employment for persons with severe mental illness. *Journal of Consulting and Clinical Psychology, 72,* 479–490.

Razzano, L. A., Cook, J. A., Burke-Miller, J. K., Mueser, K. T., Pickett-Schenk, S. A., Grey, D. D., et al. (2005). Clinical factors associated with employment among people with severe mental illness: Findings from the Employment Intervention Demonstration Program. *Journal of Nervous and Mental Disease, 193,* 705-713.

Schonebaum, A. D., Boyd, J. K., & Dudek, K. J. (2006). A comparison of competitive employment outcomes for the clubhouse and PACT models. *Psychiatric Services, 57*(10), 1416–1420.

Additional effectiveness research

Becker, D. R., & Drake, R. E. (2003). *A working life for people with severe mental illness.* New York: Oxford University Press.

Presents the research evidence for the SE model and a compelling rationale for using a recovery-oriented approach.

Bond, G. R., Resnick, S. G., Drake, R. E., Xie, H., McHugo, G. J., & Bebout, R. R. (2001). Does competitive employment improve nonvocational outcomes for people with severe mental illness? *Journal of Consulting and Clinical Psychology, 69,* 489-501.

Suggests that competitive employment for a sustained period of time is associated with improved symptoms and higher self-esteem compared to unemployment.

Drake, R. E., Becker, D. R., Clark, R. E., & Mueser, K. T. (1999). Research on the Individual Placement and Support model of supported employment. *Psychiatric Quarterly, 70,* 289-301.

Summarizes the literature on Individual Placement and Support.

Marrone, J., & Gold, M. (1994). Supported employment for people with mental illness: Myths and facts. *Journal of Rehabilitation, 60*(4), 38-47.

Addresses some misconceptions about SE.

Salyers, M. P., Becker, D. R., Drake, R. E., Torrey, W. C., & Wyzik, P. F. (2004). A ten-year follow-up of a supported employment program. *Psychiatric Services, 55,* 302-308.

Van Dongen, C. J. (1996). Quality of life and self-esteem in working and nonworking persons with mental illness. *Community Mental Health Journal, 32,* 535-548.

Suggests a positive correlation between working and both quality of life and self-esteem.

Critical ingredients

Bond, G. R. (1998). Principles of the Individual Placement and Support model: Empirical support. *Psychiatric Rehabilitation Journal, 22,* 11-23.

Summarizes the research supporting six principles of SE.

Bond, G. R. (2004). Supported employment: Evidence for an evidence-based practice. *Psychiatric Rehabilitation Journal, 27,* 345-359.

Drake, R. E., & Becker, D. R. (1996). The Individual Placement and Support model of supported employment. *Psychiatric Services, 47,* 473-475.

Summarizes the key principles of SE.

Employment Intervention Demonstration Program (EIDP). (2000). *Principles for employment services and support* [brochure]. Chicago: University of Illinois at Chicago, R & T Center.

Lists the principles of SE based on a large, multi-site demonstration project.

Gowdy, E. L., Carlson, L. S., & Rapp, C. A. (2003). Practices differentiating high-performing from low-performing supported employment programs. *Psychiatric Rehabilitation Journal, 26,* 232-239.

McGurk, S. R., & Mueser, K. T. (2003). Cognitive functioning and employment in severe mental illness. *Journal of Nervous and Mental Disease, 191,* 789-798.

Historical context for supported employment

Anthony, W. A., & Blanch, A. (1987). Supported employment for persons who are psychiatrically disabled: An historical and conceptual perspective. *Psychosocial Rehabilitation Journal, 11*(2), 5-23.

Argues for extending SE for people with developmental disabilities to people with mental illnesses.

Bond, G. R. (1992). Vocational rehabilitation. In R. P. Liberman (Ed.), *Handbook of psychiatric rehabilitation* (pp. 244-275). New York: Macmillan.

Comprehensively reviews controlled studies of vocational approaches for consumers with serious mental illnesses.

Bond, G. R., & McDonel, E. C. (1991). Vocational rehabilitation outcomes for persons with psychiatric disabilities: An update. *Journal of Vocational Rehabilitation, 1*, 9-20.

Reviews the vocational literature.

Cook, J. A., & Pickett, S. A. (1994). Recent trends in vocational rehabilitation for people with psychiatric disability. *American Rehabilitation, 20*(4), 2-12.

Reviews the vocational literature.

Harding, C. M., Strauss, J. S., Hafez, H., & Liberman, P. B. (1987). Work and mental illness. Toward an integration of the rehabilitation process. *Journal of Nervous and Mental Disease, 175*, 317-326.

Uses a well-known Vermont study to articulate the principles of rehabilitation.

Marrone, J. (1993). Creating positive vocational outcomes for people with severe mental illness. *Psychosocial Rehabilitation Journal, 17*(2), 43-62.

Provides a practical guide to various vocational alternatives.

Newman, L. (1970). Instant placement: A new model for providing rehabilitation services within a community mental health program. *Community Mental Health Journal, 6*, 401-410.

Probably the first published paper to articulate the place-train approach to SE. Published nearly two decades before its widespread adoption.

Noble, J. H., Honberg, R. S., Hall, L. L., & Flynn, L. M. (1997). *A legacy of failure: The inability of the federal-state vocational rehabilitation system to serve people with severe mental illness.* Arlington, VA: National Alliance for the Mentally Ill.

Provides a scathing analysis of the vocational rehabilitation system and the barriers to employment faced by families helping consumers with mental illnesses.

Russert, M. G., & Frey, J. L. (1991). The PACT vocational model: A step into the future. *Psychosocial Rehabilitation Journal, 14*(4), 7-18.

Presents a conceptual overview of the PACT model of employment, which has had critical influence on the evolution of the SE model.

Wehman, P., & Moon, M. S. (Eds.). (1988). *Vocational rehabilitation and supported employment.* Baltimore: Brookes Publishing Co.

Demonstrates how to implement SE for a range of disability groups.

First-person perspectives

Bailey, J. (1998). I'm just an ordinary person. *Psychiatric Rehabilitation Journal, 22*, 8-10.

A powerful first-person account of the employment process.

Caswell, J. S. (2001). Employment: A consumer's perspective. In D. R. Becker & M. Barcus (Eds.), *Connections–State partnership initiative,* Vol. Spring/Summer (p. 5). Fairfax, VA: Virginia Commonwealth University.

Rothschild, D. P. (2006). *Kiosks Keep the Devils Away.* Lincoln, NE: Universe.

Practice issues

Consumer choice

Bedell, J. R., Draving, D., Parrish, A., Gervey, R., & Guastadisegni, P. (1998). A description and comparison of experiences of people with mental disorders in supported employment and paid prevocational training. *Psychiatric Rehabilitation Journal, 21*, 279-283.

Compares preferences for competitive and sheltered employment.

Mueser, K. T., Becker, D. R., & Wolfe, R. (2001). Supported employment, job preferences, and job tenure and satisfaction. *Journal of Mental Health, 10*, 411-417.

Examines the impact of finding jobs that match the occupational choices of consumers on job retention rates.

Engaging consumers in Supported Employment

Ahrens, C. S., Frey, J. L., & Burke, S. C. (1999). An individualized job engagement approach for persons with severe mental illness. *Journal of Rehabilitation, 65*(4), 17-24.

Discusses helpful strategies for engaging consumers who do not have vocational goals.

Vocational assessment

Frey, J. L., & Godfrey, M. (1991). A comprehensive clinical vocational assessment: The PACT approach. *Journal of Applied Rehabilitation Counseling, 22*(2), 25-28.

Describes practical vocational assessment methods.

Job development

Bissonnette, D. (1994). *Beyond traditional job development: The art of creating opportunity.* Chatsworth, CA: Milt Wright.

A highly engaging, comprehensive, practical guide to strategies for developing jobs.

Gervey, R., & Kowal, R. (1995). Job development strategies for placing persons with psychiatric disabilities into supported employment jobs in a large city. *Psychosocial Rehabilitation Journal, 18*(4), 95-113.

Describes the job development experiences of one SE program.

Griffin, C. & Hammis. D. (2003). *Making self-employment work for people with disabilities.* Baltimore: Brookes Publishing Co.

Luecking, R. G., Fabian, E. S., & Tilson, G. P. (2004). *Working relationships: creating career opportunities for job seekers with disabilities through employer partnerships.* Baltimore: Brookes Publishing Co.

Reasonable accommodations and disclosure of disability

Berven, N. L., & Driscoll, J. H. (1981). The effects of past psychiatric disability on employer evaluation of a job applicant. *Journal of Applied Rehabilitation Counseling, 12,* 50-55.

Presents research that demonstrates that employers discriminate against job applicants who have psychiatric disorders.

MacDonald-Wilson, K. L, Rogers, E. S., Massaro, J. M, Lyass, A., & Crean, T. (2002). An investigation of reasonable workplace accommodations for people with psychiatric disabilities: Quantitative findings from a multi-site study. *Community Mental Health Journal, 38,* 35-50.

Provides a conceptual overview of disclosure issues in the workplace and describes commonly used accommodations for consumers with mental illnesses.

MacDonald-Wilson, K. L., & Whitman, A. (1995). Encouraging disclosure of psychiatric disability: Mental health consumer and service provider perspectives on what employers do. *American Rehabilitation, 21,* 15-19.

Mancuso, L. L. (1995). Achieving reasonable accommodation for workers with psychiatric disabilities: Understanding the employer's perspective. *American Rehabilitation, 21,* 2-8.

Analyzes reasonable accommodations for consumers with serious mental illnesses.

Job retention and career development

Baron, R. C.. & Salzer, M. S. (2000). The career patterns of persons with serious mental illness: Generating a new vision of lifetime careers for those in recovery. *American Journal of Psychiatric Rehabilitation, 4,* 136-156.

Reports the findings of a qualitative study of career aspirations of consumers with serious mental illnesses.

Cook, J. A. (1992). Job ending among youth and adults with severe mental illness. *Journal of Mental Health Administration, 19(2),* 158-169.

Describes reasons for job terminations among consumers with serious mental illnesses.

Resnick, S. G., & Bond, G. R. (2001). The Indiana Job Satisfaction Scale: Job satisfaction in vocational rehabilitation for people with serious mental illness. *Psychiatric Rehabilitation Journal, 25,* 12-19.

Reports on a study that suggests a modest association between early job satisfaction and job retention.

Implementation and administrative issues

State mental health perspective

Hogan, M. F. (1999). *Supported employment: How can mental health leaders make a difference?* Columbus, OH: Ohio Department of Mental Health.

Analyzes the role of state mental health administrators in promoting employment.

Financing and cost effectiveness of Supported Employment

Latimer, E. A. (2001). Economic impacts of supported employment for persons with severe mental illness. *Canadian Journal of Psychiatry, 46*, 496-505.

Comprehensively reviews the literature on the costs and benefits of SE.

Latimer, E. A., Bush, P. W., Becker, D. R., Drake, R. E., & Bond, G. R. (2004). The cost of high-fidelity supported employment programs for people with severe mental illness. *Psychiatric Services, 55*, 401-406.

Issues for program leaders

Balser, R., Hornby, H., Fraser, K., & McKenzie, C. (2001). *Business partnerships, employment outcomes: The Mental Health Employer Consortium.* Portland, ME: Maine Medical Center. Available through http://www.ecampus. com/bk_detail.asp?referrer=617&ISBN=075672 5860 or http://www.dianepublishingcentral.com/ ProductDetail.asp?ProductID=12004.

Presents an excellent model for partnering with local businesses regarding employing consumers with serious mental illnesses.

Becker, D. R., Torrey, W. C., Toscano, R., Wyzik, P. F., & Fox, T. S. (1998). Building recovery-oriented services: Lessons from implementing IPS in community mental health centers. *Psychiatric Rehabilitation Journal, 22*, 51-54.

Reviews the issues facing program leaders who seek to promote SE.

Ford, L. H. (1995). *Providing employment support for people with long-term mental illness: Choices, resources, and practical strategies.* Baltimore: Brookes Publishing Co.

A down-to-earth, common-sense approach to SE.

Converting day treatment to Supported Employme

McCarthy, D., Thompson, D., & Olson, S. (1998). Planning a statewide project to convert day treatment to supported employment. *Psychiatric Rehabilitation Journal, 22*, 30-33.

Provides a state mental health administrator's perspective on the issues in promoting the conversion of day treatment services to SE.

Torrey, W. C., Becker, D. R., & Drake, R. E. (1995). Rehabilitative day treatment vs. supported employment: II. Consumer, family, and staff reactions to a program change. *Psychosocial Rehabilitation Journal, 18*(3), 67-75.

Reports on one in a series of studies examining the impact on consumers and family members of converting day treatment to SE.

Torrey, W. C., Mead, S., & Ross, G. (1998). Addressing the social needs of mental health consumers when day treatment programs convert to supported employment: Can consumer-run services play a role? *Psychiatric Rehabilitation Journal, 22*, 73-75.

Examines strategies for overcoming social isolation among consumers with serious mental illnesses who obtain employment.

State vocational rehabilitation agency

Marrone, J., & Hagner, D. (1993). Getting the most from the VR system. *Tools for Inclusion, Family and Consumer Services,* (1).

Discusses strategies for maximizing assistance from the vocational rehabilitation system.

Marshak, L. E., Bostick, D., & Turton, L. J. (1990). Closure outcomes for clients with psychiatric disabilities served by the vocational rehabilitation system. *Rehabilitation Counseling Bulletin, 33*, 247-250.

Suggests that the rate of achieving vocational rehabilitation eligibility is twice as high for people with physical disabilities as it is for people with serious mental illnesses.

Barriers to employment

Braitman, A., Counts, P., Davenport, R., Zurlinden, B., Rogers, M., Clauss, J., et al. (1995). Comparison of barriers to employment for unemployed and employed clients in a case management program: An exploratory study. *Psychiatric Rehabilitation Journal, 19*, 3-8.

Suggests that most clinicians view consumers with serious mental illnesses as being unmotivated.

Lehman, A. F., & Steinwachs, D. M. (1998). Patterns of usual care for schizophrenia: Initial results from the Schizophrenia Patient Outcomes Research Team (PORT) client survey. *Schizophrenia Bulletin, 24*, 11-20.

Suggests that access to vocational services in the usual system of care is very low. Less than 25 percent of consumers in the study had any vocational goal in their treatment plan.

Rutman, I. D. (1994). How psychiatric disability expresses itself as a barrier to employment. *Psychosocial Rehabilitation Journal, 17*(3), 15-35.

Summarizes the diverse barriers to employment for consumers with serious mental illnesses.

Wahl, O. (1997, May). *Consumer experience with stigma: Results of a national survey.* Arlington, VA: National Alliance for the Mentally Ill.

Documents the pervasiveness of stigma of mental illnesses.

Walls, R. T., Dowler, D. L., & Fullmer, S. L. (1990). Incentives and disincentives to supported employment. In F. R. Rusch (Ed.), *Supported employment: Models, methods, and issues* (pp. 251-269). Sycamore, IL: Sycamore Publishing.

Describes disincentives to employment inherent in the Social Security system.

Special populations

Alverson, H., & Vincente, E. (1998). An ethnographic study of vocational rehabilitation for Puerto Rican Americans with severe mental illness. *Psychiatric Rehabilitation Journal, 22*, 69-72.

Describes the experiences of Puerto Rican Americans with serious mental illnesses who receive SE services.

Cook, J. A., Pickett-Schenk, S. A., Grey, D., Banghart, M., Rosenheck, R. A., & Randolph, F. (2001). Vocational outcomes among formerly homeless persons with severe mental illness in the ACCESS program. *Psychiatric Services, 52*, 1075-1080.

Suggests that case management and outreach services alone to homeless people with mental illnesses do not increase employment rates. Targeted job placement services do appear to make a difference.

Goering, P., Cochrane, J., Potasznik, H., Wasylenki, D., & Lancee, W. (1988). Women and work: After psychiatric hospitalization. In L. L. Bachrach & C. C. Nadelson (Eds.), *Treating chronically mentally ill women* (pp. 45-61). Washington, DC: American Psychiatric Press.

Describes the unique issues facing women with mental illnesses who seek employment.

Harris, M., Bebout, R. R., Freeman, D. W., Hobbs, M. D., Kline, J. D., Miller, S. L., et al. (1997). Work stories: Psychological responses to work in a population of dually diagnosed adults. *Psychiatric Quarterly, 68,* 131-153.

Presents a qualitative analysis of the unique issues facing consumers with co-occurring disorders of mental illness and substance use problems.

Supported Education

Carlson, L., Eichler, M. S., Huff, S., & Rapp, C. A. (2003). *A tale of two cities: Best practices in supported education.* Lawrence: The University of Kansas, School of Social Welfare.

Suggests that advancement is often associated with education and, therefore, Supported Education should always be a part of Supported Employment.

Mowbray, C. T., Brown, K. S., Furlong-Norman, K., & Soydan, A. S. (Eds.). (2002). *Supported education & psychiatric rehabilitation: Models and methods.* Linthicum, MD: International Association of Psychosocial Rehabilitation Services. Available through http://www.uspra.org.

Unger, K. V. (1998). *Handbook on supported education: Providing services for students with psychiatric disabilities.* Baltimore: Brookes Publishing Co.

Describes Supported Education for consumers with serious mental illnesses.

Implementing evidence-based practices

Drake, R. E., Merrens, M. R., & Lynde, D. W. (Eds.). (2005). *Evidence-based mental health practice: A textbook.* New York: W.W. Norton.

An excellent, readable primer for the Evidence-Based Practices (EBP) KITs. Introduces the concepts and approaches of EBP for treating serious mental illnesses and describes the importance of research in intervention science and the evolution of EBPs. A chapter for each of five EBPs provides historical background, practice principles, and an introduction to implementation. Vignettes highlight the experiences of staff and consumers.

Drake, R. E., Goldman, H. H., Leff, H. S., Lehman, A. F., Dixon, L., Mueser, K. T., et al. (2001). Implementing evidence-based practices in routine mental health service settings. *Psychiatric Services, 52,* 179-182.

Defines the differences between evidence-based practices and related concepts, such as guidelines and algorithms. Discusses common concerns about using EBPs, such as whether ethical values have a role in shaping such practices and how to deal with clinical situations for which no scientific evidence exists.

Fixsen, D. L., Naoom, S. F., Blase, K. A., Friedman, R. M., & Wallace, F. (2005). *Implementation Research: A synthesis of the literature. (FMHI Publication No. 231).* Tampa, FL: University of South Florida, Louis de la Parte Florida Mental Health Institute, The National Implementation Research Network. Available through http://nirn.fmhi.usf.edu.

Goldman, H. H., Ganju, V., Drake, R. E., Gorman, P., Hogan, M., Hyde, P. S., et al. (2001). Policy implications for implementing evidence-based practices. *Psychiatric Services, 52,* 1591-1597.

Describes the policy and administrative issues related to implementing evidence-based practices, particularly in public-sector settings.

Hyde, P. S., Falls, K., Morris, J. A., & Schoenwald, S. K. (2003). *Turning knowledge into practice: A manual for behavioral health administrators and practitioners about understanding and implementing evidence-based practices.* Boston: Technical Assistance Collaborative. Available through http://www.tacinc.org/Docs/HS/EPBmanual.pdf.

Torrey, W. C., Drake, R. E., Dixon, L., Burns, B. J., Flynn, L., Rush, A. J., et al. (2001). Implementing evidence-based practices for persons with severe mental illnesses. *Psychiatric Services, 52,* 45-50.

Summarizes perspectives on how best to change and sustain effective practice. Includes a sample plan for implementing EBPs.

Additional readings for program leaders and public mental health authorities

Batalden, P. B., & Stoltz, P. K. (1993). A framework for the continual improvement of health care: Building and applying professional and improvement knowledge to test changes in daily work. *The Joint Commission Journal on Quality Improvement, 19,* 424-447.

Gowdy, E., & Rapp, C. A. (1989). Managerial behavior: The common denominators of successful community based programs. *Psychosocial Rehabilitation Journal, 13*(2), 31-51.

Nelson, E. C., Batalden, P. B., & Ryer, J. C. (Eds.). (1998). *Clinical improvement action guide.* Oakbrook Terrace, IL: Joint Commission on Accreditation of Healthcare Organizations.

Rapp, C. A. (1993). Client-centered performance management and the inverted hierarchy. In R. W. Flexer & P. L. Solomon (Eds.), *Community and social support for people with severe mental disabilities* (pp. 173–192). Boston: Andover.

Rapp, C. A. (1998). Supportive case management context: Creating the conditions for effectiveness. In C. A. Rapp (Author), *The strengths model: Case management with people suffering from severe and persistent mental illness* (pp.163-193). New York: Oxford University Press.

Supervisor's Tool Box. (1997). Lawrence: University of Kansas, School of Social Welfare.

EVIDENCE-BASED
PRACTICES
KIT

Knowledge Informing Transformation

The Evidence

References

The following list includes the references for all citations in the KIT.

Becker, D. R., Bond, G. R., McCarthy, D., Thompson, D., Xie, H., McHugo, G. J., et al. (2001). Converting day treatment centers to supported employment programs in Rhode Island. *Psychiatric Services, 52*, 351-357.

Becker, D. R., Smith, J., Tanzman, B., Drake, R. E., & Tremblay, T. (2001). Fidelity of supported employment programs and employment outcomes. *Psychiatric Services, 52*, 834-836.

Bond, G. R., & Salyers, M. P. (2004). Prediction of outcome from the Dartmouth Assertive Community Treatment Fidelity Scale. *CNS Spectrums, 9*, 937-942.

Bond, G. R., Vogler, K. M., Resnick, S. G., Evans, L. J., Drake, R. E., & Becker, D. R. (2001). Dimensions of supported employment: Factor structure of the IPS Fidelity Scale. *Journal of Mental Health, 10*, 383-393.

Bond, G. R., Becker, D. R., Drake, R. E., Rapp, C. A., Meisler, N., Lehman, A. F., et al. (2001). Implementing supported employment as an evidence-based practice. *Psychiatric Services, 52*, 313-322.

Bond, G. R., Drake, R. E., Mueser. K. T., & Becker, D. R. (1997). An update on supported employment for people with severe mental illness. *Psychiatric Services, 48*, 335-346.

Bond, G. R., Becker, D. R., Drake, R. E., & Vogler, K. M. (1997). A fidelity scale for the Individual Placement and Support model of supported employment. *Rehabilitation Counseling Bulletin, 40*, 265-284.

Bond, G. R., Dietzen, L. L., Vogler, K., Katuin, C. H., McGrew, J. H., & Miller, L. D. (1995). Toward a framework for evaluating cost and benefits of psychiatric rehabilitation: Three case examples. *Journal of Vocational Rehabilitation, 5*, 75-88.

Campbell, J. & Schraiber, R. (1989, Summer). *The Well-Being Project: Mental health clients speak for themselves.* Sacramento: California Network of Mental Health Clients. Available from the California Network of Mental Health Clients, 1722 J Street, Suite 324, Sacramento, CA 95814.

Clark, R. E. (1998). Supported employment and managed care: Can they coexist? *Psychiatric Rehabilitation Journal, 22*, 62-68.

Cook, J. A., Leff, H. S., Blyler, C. R., Gold, P. B., Goldberg, R. W., Mueser, K. T., et al. (2005). Results of a multisite randomized trial of supported employment interventions for individuals with severe mental illness. *Archives of General Psychiatry, 62*, 505-512.

Ganju, V. (2004, June). *Evidence-based practices: Responding to the challenge.* Presented at the NASMHPD Commissioner's Meeting, San Francisco, CA.

Hyde, P. S., Falls, K., Morris, J. A., & Schoenwald, S. K. (2003). Turning knowledge into practice: A manual for behavioral health administrators and practitioners about understanding and implementing evidence-based practices. Boston: Technical Assistance Collaborative Available through http://www.tacinc.org.

Institute of Medicine (2006). Improving the quality of health care for mental and substance-use conditions: Quality Chasm Series. Washington, DC: National Academy of Sciences.

Luecking, R. G., Fabian, E. S., & Tilson, G. P. (2004). *Working relationships: creating career opportunities for job seekers with disabilities through employer partnerships* (p. 54). Baltimore: Brookes Publishing Co.

McQuilken, M., Zahniser, J. H., Novak, J., Starks, R. D., Olmos, A., & Bond, G. R. (2003). The work project survey: Consumer perspectives on work. *Journal of Vocational Rehabilitation, 18*, 59-68.

Mueser, K. T., Becker, D. R.; Torrey, W. C., Xie, H., Drake, R. E., Bond, G. R.. et al. (1997). Work and nonvocational domains of functioning in persons with severe mental illness: A longitudinal analysis. *Journal of Nervous and Mental Disease. 185*:419-426.

Mueser, K. T., Becker, D. R., & Wolfe, R. (2001). Supported employment, job preferences, job tenure and satisfaction. *Journal of Mental Health, 10*, 411-417.

Mueser, K. T., Salyers, M. P. & Mueser, P.R. (2001). A prospective analysis of work in schizophrenia. *Schizophrenia Bulletin, 27,* 281-296

National Advisory Mental Health Council Workgroup on Child and Adolescent Mental Health Intervention Development and Deployment. (2001). *Blueprint for change: research on child and adolescent mental health.* Rockville, MD: National Institute of Mental Health. Available through http://www.nimh.nih.gov.

New Freedom Commission on Mental Health. (2003). *Achieving the promise: Transforming mental health care in America. Final Report.* (DHHS Publication. No. SMA-03-3832). Rockville. MD: Author.

Peters, T. J., & Waterman, R. H. (1982). *In search of excellence.* New York: Harper & Row.

Rogers, E. S., Walsh, D., Massotta, L., & Danley, D. (1991). *Massachusetts survey of client preferences for community support services. Final report.* Boston: Center for Psychiatric Rehabilitation.

Shaheen, G., Williams, F., and Dennis D. (Eds.). (2003). *Work as a priority: A resource for employing people who have serious mental illness and who are homeless.* (DHHS Publication. No. SMA 03-3834). Rockville, MD: Center for Mental Health Services, Substance Abuse and Mental Health Services Administration. Available through http://www.samhsa.gov.

Teague, G. R., Drake, R. E., & Ackerson, T. H. (1995). Evaluating use of continuous treatment teams for persons with mental illness and substance abuse. *Psychiatric Services, 46,* 689-695.

Twamley, E. W., Jeste, D. V., & Lehman, A. F. (2003). Vocational rehabilitation in schizophrenia and other psychotic disorders: A literature review and meta-analysis of randomized controlled trials. *Journal of Nervous and Mental Disease, 191,* 515-523.

U.S. Department of Health and Human Services. (1999). *Mental health: A report of the surgeon general.* Rockville, MD: U.S. Department of Health and Human Services, Substance Abuse and Mental Health Services Administration, Center for Mental Health Services, and National Institutes of Health, National Institute of Mental Health.

U.S. Department of Health and Human Services. (2001). *Mental health: Culture, race, and ethnicity. A supplement to mental health: A report of the surgeon general.* Rockville, MD: U.S. Department of Health and Human Services, Substance Abuse and Mental Health Services Administration, Center for Mental Health Services.

Smith, G., Kennedy, C., Knipper, S., & O'Brien, J. (2005). Using Medicaid to support working age adults with serious mental illnesses in the community: A Handbook. Washington, D.C.: U.S. Department of Health and Human Services, Office of the Assistant Secretary of Planning and Evaluation.

Uttaro T., & Mechanic D (1994). The NAMI consumer survey analysis of unmet needs. *Hospital and Community Psychiatry, 45,* 372–374.

EVIDENCE-BASED
PRACTICES
KiT

Knowledge Informing Transformation

The Evidence

Acknowledgments

The materials included in the Supported Employment KIT were developed through the National Implementing Evidence-Based Practices Project. The Project's Coordinating Center—the New Hampshire-Dartmouth Psychiatric Research Center—in partnership with many other collaborators, including clinicians, researchers, consumers, family members, and administrators, and operating under the direction of the Substance Abuse and Mental Health Services Administration, Center for Mental Health Services, developed, evaluated, and revised these materials.

We wish to acknowledge the many people who contributed to all aspects of this project. In particular, we wish to acknowledge the contributors and consultants on the next few pages.

SAMHSA Center for Mental Health Services, Oversight Committee

Michael English
Division of Service and Systems Improvement
Rockville, Maryland

Neal B. Brown
Community Support Programs Branch
Division of Service and Systems Improvement
Rockville, Maryland

Sandra Black
Community Support Programs Branch
Division of Service and Systems Improvement
Rockville, Maryland

Crystal R. Blyler
Community Support Programs Branch
Division of Service and Systems Improvement
Rockville, Maryland

Pamela Fischer
Homeless Programs Branch
Division of Service and Systems Improvement
Rockville, Maryland

Sushmita Shoma Ghose
Community Support Programs Branch
Division of Service and Systems Improvement
Rockville, Maryland

Patricia Gratton
Division of Service and Systems Improvement
Rockville, Maryland

Betsy McDonel Herr
Community Support Programs Branch
Division of Service and Systems Improvement
Rockville, Maryland

Larry D. Rickards
Homeless Programs Branch
Division of Service and Systems Improvement
Rockville, Maryland

Co-Leaders

Deborah Becker
Dartmouth Psychiatric Research Center
Lebanon, New Hampshire

Gary R. Bond
Indiana University–Purdue University
Indianapolis, Indiana

Contributors

Charity Appell
Ascutney, Vermont

Morris D. Bell
Veteran's Administration
West Haven, Connecticut

Crystal R. Blyler
Community Support Programs Branch
Division of Service and Systems Improvement
Rockville, Maryland

Randee Chafkin
U.S. Department of Labor
Washington, D.C.

Michael J. Cohen
National Alliance on Mental Illness (NAMI)
Concord, New Hampshire

Efrain Diaz
Newington, Connecticut

Cathy Donahue
Calais, Vermont

Kana Enomoto
Substance Abuse and Mental Health Services
Administration
Rockville, Maryland

Erik Johannessen
Odyssey
Hampton, New Hampshire

Jeffrey Krolick
Options for Southern Oregon
Grants Pass, Oregon

David W. Lynde
Dartmouth Psychiatric Research Center
Concord, New Hampshire

Doug Marty
The University of Kansas
Lawrence, Kansas

Gregory J. McHugo
Dartmouth Psychiatric Research Center
Lebanon, New Hampshire

Alan C. McNabb
Ascutney, Vermont

Matthew Merrens
Dartmouth Psychiatric Research Center
Lebanon, New Hampshire

Bill Naughton
Southeastern Mental Health Authority
Norich, Connecticut

Ernest Quimby
Howard University
Washington, D.C.

Charles A. Rapp
The University of Kansas
Lawrence, Kansas

Dennis Ross
Marshfield, Vermont

Gary Shaheen
Advocates for Human Potential, Inc.
Albany, New York

Karin Swain
Dartmouth Psychiatric Research Center
Lebanon, New Hampshire

Boyd J. Tracy
Dartmouth Psychiatric Research Center
Rutland, Vermont

William Torrey
Dartmouth Medical School
Hanover, New Hampshire

Consultants to the National Implementing Evidence-Based Practices Project

Dan Adams
St. Johnsbury, Vermont

Diane C. Alden
New York State Office of Mental Health
New York, New York

Lindy Fox Amadio
Dartmouth Psychiatric Research Center
Concord, New Hampshire

Diane Asher
University of Kansas
Lawrence, Kansas

Stephen R. Baker
University of Maryland School of Medicine
Baltimore, Maryland

Stephen T. Baron
Department of Mental Health
Washington, D.C.

Deborah R. Becker
Dartmouth Psychiatric Research Center
Lebanon, New Hampshire

Nancy L. Bolton
Cambridge, Massachusetts

Patrick E. Boyle
Case Western Reserve University
Cleveland, Ohio

Mike Brady
Adult & Child Mental Health Center
Indianapolis, Indiana

Ken Braiterman
National Alliance on Mental Illness (NAMI)
Concord, New Hampshire

Janice Braithwaite
Snow Hill, Maryland

Michael Brody
Southwest Connecticut Mental Health Center
Bridgeport, Connecticut

Mary Brunette
Dartmouth Psychiatric Research Center
Concord, New Hampshire

Sharon Bryson
Ashland, Oregon

Barbara J. Burns
Duke University School of Medicine
Durham, North Carolina

Jennifer Callaghan
University of Kansas
School of Social Welfare
Lawrence, Kansas

Kikuko Campbell
Indiana University–Purdue University
Indianapolis, Indiana

Linda Carlson
University of Kansas
Lawrence, Kansas

Diana Chambers
Department of Health Services
Burlington, Vermont

Alice Claggett
University of Toledo College of Medicine
Toledo, Ohio

Marilyn Cloud
Department of Health and Human Services
Concord, New Hampshire

Melinda Coffman
University of Kansas
Lawrence, Kansas

Jon Collins
Office of Mental Health and Addiction Services
Salem, Oregon

Laurie Coots
Dartmouth Psychiatric Research Center
Lebanon, New Hampshire

Judy Cox
New York State Office of Mental Health
New York, New York

Harry Cunningham
Dartmouth Psychiatric Research Center
Concord, New Hampshire

Gene Deegan
University of Kansas
Lawrence, Kansas

Natalie DeLuca
Indiana University – Purdue University
Indianapolis, Indiana

Robert E. Drake
Dartmouth Psychiatric Research Center
Lebanon, New Hampshire

Molly Finnerty
New York State Office of Mental Health
New York, New York

Laura Flint
Dartmouth Evidence Based Practices Center
Burlington, Vermont

Vijay Ganju
National Association of State Mental Health
Program Directors Research Institute
Alexandria, Virginia

Susan Gingerich
Narberth, Pennsylvania

Phillip Glasgow
Wichita, Kansas

Howard H. Goldman
University of Maryland School of Medicine
Baltimore, Maryland

Paul G. Gorman
Dartmouth Psychiatric Research Center
Lebanon, New Hampshire

Gretchen Grappone
Concord, New Hampshire

Eileen B. Hansen
University of Maryland School of Medicine
University of Maryland, Baltimore

Kathy Hardy
Strafford, Vermont

Joyce Hedstrom
Courtland, Kansas

Lon Herman
Department of Mental Health
Columbus, Ohio

Lia Hicks
Adult & Child Mental Health Center
Indianapolis, Indiana

Debra Hrouda
Case Western Reserve University
Cleveland, Ohio

Bruce Jensen
Indiana University–Purdue University
Indianapolis, Indiana

Clark Johnson
Salem, New Hampshire

Amanda M. Jones
Indiana University – Purdue University
Indianapolis, Indiana

Joyce Jorgensen
Department of Health and Human Services
Concord, New Hampshire

Hea-Won Kim
Indiana University – Purdue University
Indianapolis, Indiana

David A. Kime
Transcendent Visions and Crazed Nation Zines
Fairless Hills, Pennsylvania

Dale Klatzker
The Providence Center
Providence, Rhode Island

Kristine Knoll
Dartmouth Psychiatric Research Center
Lebanon, New Hampshire

Bill Krenek
Department of Mental Health
Columbus, Ohio

Rick Kruszynski
Case Western Reserve University
Cleveland, Ohio

H. Stephen Leff
The Evaluation Center at the Human Services
Research Institute
Cambridge, Massachusetts

Treva E. Lichti
National Association on Mental Illness (NAMI)
Wichita, Kansas

Wilma J. Lutz
Ohio Department of Mental Health
Columbus, Ohio

Anthony D. Mancini
New York State Office of Mental Health
New York, New York

Paul Margolies
Hudson River Psychiatric Center
Poughkeepsie, New York

Tina Marshall
University of Maryland School of Medicine
Baltimore, Maryland

Ann McBride (deceased)
Oklahoma City, Oklahoma

William R. McFarlane
Maine Medical Center
Portland, Maine

Mike McKasson
Adult & Child Mental Health Center
Indianapolis, Indiana

Alan C. McNabb
Ascutney, Vermont

Meka McNeal
University of Maryland School of Medicine
Baltimore, Maryland

Ken Minkoff
ZiaLogic
Albuquerque, New Mexico

Michael W. Moore
Office of Mental Health and Addiction Services
Salem, Oregon

Roger Morin
The Center for Health Care Services
San Antonio, Texas

Lorna Moser
Indiana University–Purdue University
Indianapolis, Indiana

Kim T. Mueser
Dartmouth Psychiatric Research Center
Concord, New Hampshire

Britt J. Myrhol
New York State Office of Mental Health
New York, New York

Bill Naughton
Southeastern Mental Health Authority
Norwich, Connecticut

Nick Nichols
Department of Health
Burlington, Vermont

Bernard F. Norman
Northeast Kingdom Human Services
Newport, Vermont

Linda O'Malia
Oregon Health and Science University
Portland, Oregon

Ruth O. Ralph
University of Southern Maine
Portland, Maine

Angela L. Rollins
Indian University–Purdue University
Indianapolis, Indiana

Tony Salerno
New York State Office of Mental Health
New York, New York

Diana C. Seybolt
University of Maryland School of Medicine
Baltimore, Maryland

Patricia W. Singer
Santa Fe, New Mexico

Mary Kay Smith
University of Toledo
Toledo, Ohio

Diane Sterenbuch
Bethesda, Maryland

Bette Stewart
University of Maryland School of Medicine
Baltimore, Maryland

Steve Stone
Mental Health and Recovery Board
Ashland, Ohio

Maureen Sullivan
Department of Health and Human Services
Concord, New Hampshire

Beth Tanzman
Vermont Department of Health
Burlington, Vermont

Greg Teague
University of Southern Florida
Tampa, Florida

Boyd J. Tracy
Dartmouth Psychiatric Research Center
Lebanon, New Hampshire

Laura Van Tosh
Olympia, Washington

Joseph A. Vero
National Association on Mental Illness (NAMI)
Aurora, Ohio

Barbara L. Wieder
Case Western Reserve University
Cleveland, Ohio

Mary Woods
Westbridge Community Services
Manchester, New Hampshire

Special thanks to

The following organizations for their generous contributions:

- Johnson & Johnson
- The Robert Wood Johnson Foundation
- The John D. & Catherine T. MacArthur Foundation
- West Family Foundation

Production, editorial, and graphics support

Carolyn Boccella Bagin
Center for Clear Communication, Inc.
Rockville, Maryland

Sushmita Shoma Ghose
Westat
Rockville, Maryland

Chandria Jones
Westat
Rockville, Maryland

Tina Marshall
Gaithersburg, Maryland

Mary Anne Myers
Westat
Rockville, Maryland

Robin Ritter
Westat
Rockville, Maryland

DHHS Publication No. SMA-08-4364
Printed 2009

24768.0409.7765020404

A Life in the Community for Everyone

SAMHSA

Substance Abuse and Mental Health Services Administration
U.S. Department of Health and Human Services

Lightning Source UK Ltd.
Milton Keynes UK
UKHW050200210521
384056UK00020B/359